CAITHNESS LIFE

The motor yacht *Pathfinder* glides majestically into Wick Harbour in 1933. It was commandeered during World War Two and eventually was sunk in the Minch. *Submitted by Islay MacLeod, Thrumster Estate.*

Rescue! Crew members from the Royal Yacht *Britannia* being hauled to safety by Jimmy Coghill (leaning out of boat) and George Mackay at
sailors were in the sea? Ah, that's another story...

CONTENTS

rwick Bay in the early 1960s. How come the
Submitted by James Coghill of Murkle.

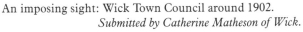

An imposing sight: Wick Town Council around 1902.
Submitted by Catherine Matheson of Wick.

George Matheson and his mother photographed prior to the First World War. George was born into a crofting family at Upper Gills, Canisbay, and was quite a remarkable individual. He invented and developed radio direction-finder for shipping which operated on the basis that the receiver was free to rotate so that it could align with the direction of the incoming signal. George died in Dunbar Hospital in 1974.

Submitted by Catherine Matheson of Wick.

Wick's Boat Day procession (in support of the local lifeboat) on January 3rd, 1916. Various organisations supported the lifeboat and prohibitionists were clearly among them as their banner reads, 'We'll Check the Liquor Traffic.' The procession appears to be going up Northcote Street from the main road. *Submitted by Catherine Matheson of Wick.*

The siblings Jack, Dorothy and May Bremner at the Trinkie outdoor pool on a windy day in early 1982. For years they ran a grocer's shop in Huddart Street, Wick. *Submitted by Graeme Dickson of Wick.*

James Bremner's 'lemonade lorry' outside his home in Huddart Street during the 1930s. The young delivery man in front is unknown.   *Submitted by Graeme Dickson of Wick.*

Fizzy soft drinks were once manufactured in Wick. Here is James Bremner, who started the business, with his wife and a friend at the Forth Bridge sometime in the 1920s.

Submitted by Graeme Dickson of Wick.

The road at Oldhall under construction in the 1940s.
Submitted by Graeme Dickson of Wick.

Brothers Jack (standing) and James Bremner prepare for the Great War. Jack was to be killed but James survived to return to Wick and set up the lemonade factory in Rutherford Street.

Submitted by Graeme Dickson of Wick.

63 Huddart Street, Wick, in the late 1890s.   *Submitted by Graeme Dickson of Wick.*

The staff of Woolworths at their annual staff dance in 1957.   *Submitted by Graeme Dickson, Wick.*

Girls on a picnic at Reay in 1936. Back row, left to right: Sheila Ross, Jessica Bain, Margaret Tait, Ella Henderson. Front: Merly Mackay, Violet Cormack and Isobel Wares.   *Submitted by Catherine Matheson of Wick.*

Some of the adults on the same picnic at Reay in 1936. William Bremner sits besides his wife Elizabeth, while Ella Tait and Elizabeth Cook squeeze in. The little one is Violet Cormack. William Bremner wrote for many years as 'Norseman' in the *Groat*.
Submitted by Catherine Matheson of Wick.

Alexander Matheson – better known as 'Sheds' – was born in 1886. As his sharp features perhaps indicate, he was a wit with a gregarious personality. His favourite mode of transport was his bicycle with which he would commute regularly between Canisbay and Wick. He died a tragic death in a house fire at Gills. When asked why he had not attended a neighbour's funeral he replied, 'Because he'll certainly no' be coming to mine.'

Submitted by Catherine Matheson.

The year is 1936 and John Green and Richard Mackenzie from John O'Groats are both in the naval reserve, standing behind William Cormack of Auckengill from HMS *Orion*. All three survived World War Two.

Submitted by Catherine Matheson of Wick.

Sisters Catherine (standing) and Mary Bremner. Catherine and her husband John Budge had a bakery in Grant Street, Wick, whilst Mary and her husband Daniel Budge ran the Thurso lemonade factory. *Submitted by Graeme Dickson of Wick.*

At Wick's North Baths in the 1930s. The North Baths have been established for 100 years now, and thanks to the Friends of the North Baths and the Trinkie they have been brought back into use in recent times. *Submitted by Graeme Dickson of Wick.*

At the Trinkie in the 1930s. On really fine days the place could be thronged and ice-cream sellers would enjoy a roaring trade. *Submitted by Graeme Dickson.*

A glorious summer day at the Trinkie pool outside Wick. Not all the work had yet been completed. We are reliably informed that the water at the Trinkie is much warmer than it looks... *Submitted by Graeme Dickson of Wick.*

This is part of the construction work on the Trinkie. The opening ceremony took place in 1931, although the pool had been used during its construction phase. The wooden rail track in the foreground was connected to the seven quarries that were opened in the area – mainly to facilitate local housing developments. *Submitted by Graeme Dickson.*

There is a romance in steam that simply is not there with modern diesel vessels, even if the fishing puffer does blow smoke across this view of Wick Harbour. *Submitted by Graeme Dickson.*

The stack yard at No. 6 Skaill (by Thurso) during the great January snowstorm of 1955.

Submitted by Mrs Elsie Mackenzie of Nybster.

A glorious harvest time in 1934. The picture shows John Begg and his family.

Submitted by Mrs Elsie Mackenzie of Nybster.

A picnic at Dounreay school in 1945 celebrating the end of World War Two. *Submitted by Mrs Elsie Mackenzie of Nybster.*

ROCKS THAT RISE IN GIDDY GRANDEUR
CLIFFS WHERE DWELT THE EAGLE GRAY
CHASMS, CAVES WHERE WILD WAVES WANDER
FORM THE CHARMS OF DUNCANSBAY

THE STACKS OF DUNCANSBAY, JOHN O' GROAT

Rocks that rise in giddy grandeur,
Cliffs where dwelt the eagle gray,
Chasms, caves where wild waves wander,
Form the charms of Duncansby.

Submitted by Mrs Elsie Mackenzie of Nybster.

Are they going to throw snowballs at their mother? Alistair and Andrew Sinclair threaten to do so in the early 1960s when Wick River was frozen over.
Submitted by Alistair Sinclair of Wick.

The ACF in 1964. Back row, left to right: William Smith, Angie Macaulay, Alistair Sutherland, Alistair Campbell and Gordon Cook. Front row: George Ross, Dennis Bremner and Alistair Mackenzie. *Submitted by Alistair Mackenzie of Wick.*

The Thurso Territorial camp at Burghead on the Moray Firth in 1912. *Submitted by Elizabeth Munro of Freswick.*

Sergeant James Sutherland of the Thurso Company of the 1st Caithness Royal Garrison Artillery. The photograph was taken shortly before the company disbanded in 1908. *Submitted by Elizabeth Munro of Freswick.*

This view of Wick town centre was probably taken in the early 1900s. *Submitted by J. Gunn of Wick.*

Remember when cars were allowed both ways on the cobbled High Street of Wick? *Submitted by Alistair Sinclair of Wick.*

Bill Mackay the butcher with his van.
Submitted by Lynsay Macadie of Wick.

So, let's be clear about this: Caithness did not want Nirex then? These banners and placards were prepared for the Caithness Against Nuclear Dumping campaign group in the 1990s.
Submitted by J. Gunn of Wick.

A venerable trio and a young lad at Stroma Harbour; the date might have been before 1900. Left to right: 'Jonnag' Innes, Gills; James Dunnet, Gills; George Wares; and young George Robertson.

Submitted by William Magee of Lower Gills.

Alan Macadie, James Macadie and George Campbell look comfortable in the saddle in 1963.

Submitted by Keith Macadie.

John MacDonald at Upper Gills on his motorbike in 1948.
Submitted by Mrs Nan Fraser of Canisbay.

Clair Fraser with his bike at Upper Gills in 1943.
Submitted by Nan Fraser of Canisbay.

Ack MacDonald at Upper Gills on his Royal Enfield in 1947.
Submitted by Mrs Nan Fraser of Canisbay.

Clair Fraser with his Chevy lorry at Upper Gills in 1944.
Submitted by Mrs Nan Fraser of Canisbay.

The big day for William Dunnet and Jessie Kennedy. The new Mrs Dunnet is wearing a wedding dress whose 1920s fashion is now in again.   *Submitted by William Magee of Lower Gills.*

Nan and Clair Fraser facing the future together on their wedding day at the registry office in Wick.

Submitted by William Magee of Lower Gills.

Har and Clair Fraser working the land at Westerloch in 1938.   *Submitted by Mrs Nan Fraser.*

From left to right: A. Harrold, G. Mackay and J. Harrold exploring the great outdoors in 1955. *Submitted anonymously.*

A day out at Thurso in 1956. Left to right: M. Sinclair, I. Bain, J. Rosie, A. Bruce, N. Harrold and N. Mackay.

Submitted anonymously.

Argyle Square, Wick, in 1907.   *Submitted by Graeme Dickson of Wick.*

Railway Station, Lybster

The railway station at Lybster at the turn of the 19th century.   *Submitted by Graeme Dickson of Wick.*

Packing herring in a firkin during the
1930s. This time-honoured activity is being
undertaken by Daniel Bethune at Dunbeath.
Submitted by Hazel Lindsay of Dunbeath.

A grand parade through Wick in 1907.

Submitted by Graeme Dickson of Wick.

The Brubster picnic of 1948. Was that a touch of sun in the picture?
Submitted by Mrs Rosalind Falconer of Halkirk.

Launching ceremony at Ackergill in 1907.

Submitted by Graeme Dickson.

A train gets caught in deep snow in 1907.

Submitted by Graeme Dickson of Wick.

Berriedale, from the Castle

Berriedale village in 1906.

Submitted by Graeme Dickson of Wick.

CHIEF MARSHAL
LIFEBOAT PROCESSION WICK JAN 3 1910

The chief marshal of the Wick lifeboat procession in 1910.

Submitted by Graeme Dickson of Wick.

The marriage of Michael Harmsworth to Jessamine at Westminster Cathedral on a dreich day in November 1937.

Submitted by Islay MacLeod of Thrumster Estate.

Donald Sutherland (born in 1836) was a shoemaker, crofter and fisherman. In 1857 he married Anne Grant (born 1839). The date of the photo is unknown but it could have been taken in the 1880s.

Submitted by Murdo Steven.

A Labour Party sale of work in the early 1960s.   *Submitted by Murdo Steven.*

The harbour has played a vital part in the economic and social history of the Royal Burgh of Wick, and in 1979 Wick Harbour Trust celebrated its centenary. Members are pictured in the town hall. Back row, from left: Captain Hamish Moore, harbour master; Councillor David Rudhall; Tom Buick, solicitor; John Lidderdale; Donnie Shearer; Edward Atkins; and William Sinclair. Front row: Donald Harper; Donald Mackay; Alistair Mackenzie; Councillor Anderson Murray, chairman; Councillor Jim Oag; John Malcolm; and James Sutherland.

Say Cheese!

A Wick High School class in the late 1950s. The teacher's name is not known. Back row, from left: Mina Miller, Mary Rosie, Sheena Sutherland, unknown, Jean Henderson, Bobby Flett, Fred Harper, James Lyall, unknown, Betty Beesley, Barbara Gunn, unknown. Middle row: Fay Fraser, Margaret Ross, ? Elder, Dede Swanson, Sheila Bremner, Christine Mowat, Betty Bremner, Eileen ?, unknown, Nettie Sutherland, Marchia Dea, Audrey Durrand. Front row: Margaret Henderson, Helen Shepherd, Catherine and Margaret Wilson, Joyce Cowie, Lorraine Mackay, Ettie Mackay, Ida Lemon, Marie Farquhar, Muriel McAdie, Agnes Bain and Hilda Bruce.

Submitted by Mrs Marie Sinclair of Wick.

Pupils at Dunbeath school in the mid-1950s.

Submitted by Murdo Steven.

Dounreay school in 1928. Back row, left to right: ? Gunn, G. Henderson, G. Mackay, D. Innes, W. Bruce, D. Shearer, H. Henderson and S. Wilson. Middle row: J. Begg, S. Mackay, J. Shearer, C. Bannerman, B. Begg and M. Begg. Seated: G. Shearer, N. Gunn, I. Begg. C. Mackay, C. Begg, E. Begg and B. Ross. Front: J. Bannerman, unknown and S. Gunn. *Submitted by Mr C. Budge of Nybster.*

Dounreay school again, this time in 1934. Back row, left to right: H. MacDonald, S. Gunn, C. Shearer, J. Galleitch, C. Begg, G. Shearer, E. Begg, J. Mackay and Miss C. MacIvor (teacher). Middle row: S. Shearer, H. Macadie, B. Ross, M. Gunn, L. Henderson, K. Mackay, K. MacDonald, W. Mackay and A. Mackay. Front: D. Gunn, M. Mackay, J. Macadie, M. Allan, I. Mackay, C. Manson, B. MacDonald, C. Allan and O. Henderson. *Submitted by C. Budge of Nybster.*

Castletown school in 1950. Back row, left to right: Gavin Younger, George Campbell, Donnie Campbell, William Stewart, William Taylor, David Swanson, Donald Macleod, Angus Macleod, William George Coghill, Alexander Hossack, James Gunn, James Taylor, Robert Keith, Keith Murray, Terence Mowat, George Anderson and Benjamin Geddes. Front row: Jeanette Farquhar, Anne Moodie, Marianne Mackay, Nellie MacDonald, Catherine Keith, Myra Ross, Catherine Crowden, Margaret MacLeod, Eleanor Christie, Elizabeth Mowat, Annette Steven, Margaret Henderson, Mary Gunn, Jean Lyall, Sheila Mackenzie, Christine Gunn and Rosemary Noble. The teacher is Miss Cameron. *Submitted by Mrs S. Keith of Castletown.*

Keiss Sunday School children assembling besides the 'Tin Kirk' in the 1920s *Submitted anonymously.*

A Pulteneytown Academy class in 1961. Back row, left to right: William Leith, Alan Miller, Graham Tait, Gavin Dunnett, unknown, Alexander Campbell, Alistair Sinclair, Ian Brown, Ronald Mackay and David Rosie. Middle row: Don Lyall, Stewart More, John Macgregor, Fiona Campbell, Elizabeth Macgregor, J. Harper, Ruth Sutherland, Isobel MacPhee, John Begg, James Rosie and William Grant. Front row: Helen Grant, Rennie Irodenko, Janet Mackay, Ann Geddes, Margaret Bissett, Moira Russell, unknown, Elizabeth Mortimer, Joan Green, Catherine Crawford, Sandra Caldwell and Mary Durrand.   *Submitted by Alistair Sinclair of Wick.*

A Castletown class in 1954. Back row, left to right: J. Crowden, D. Sutherland, W. Rosie, A. Sutherland, J. McPhee and J. McCarthy. Front row: S. Thompson, J. Campbell, M. Clyne, M. McLeod, J. Sutherland and J. Stewart.   *Submitted by Sandra Coghill of Bower.*

A picture from 1936 showing a class at Freswick. Back row, left to right: Robert Henderson, Alexander Cormack, James Henderson, Peter Miller, Donald Ross, William Cormack and teacher Miss Grant. Middle row: Clara Henderson, Isabel Wares, Sheila Ross, Margaret Tait, Merly Mackay and Barry Henderson. Front row: Nell Henderson, Violet Cormack and Margaret Henderson.

Submitted by Mrs Catherine Matheson of Auckengill.

This picture of Keiss school is believed to have been taken in 1929. Back row, from left to right: Miss Budge (teacher), Mr Sutherland (teacher), B. Sutherland, M. Sinclair, G. Cormack, S. Swanson, J. Rosie, M. Gunn and Miss Grant (teacher). Second row: C. Dunnet, D. Miller, T. Cormack, B. Sutherland, I. Miller, N. Gunn and unknown. Third row: S. Anderson, M. Steven, A. Charleston, unknown, J. Charleston and unknown. Front: unknown, A. Anderson, unknown and B. Swanson   *Submitted anonymously.*

Dunbeath school in the 1920s. Back row, left to right: Jessie MacKenzie, Jessie Sinclair, Jean Munro, Louisa MacDonald, Jennifer Gunn and Mary Hewson. Middle row, left to right: John Mackay, John Sutherland, Robert Horne, Joseph Mackay and James Cowie. Front row, left to right: Cecil Kennedy, Hugh Grant, Margaret Maclean, Annie Turner, Elizabeth Sutherland, Jessie Mackenzie, Margaret Sinclair, Teanie Horne and Margaret Gunn.   *Submitted by Murdo Steven.*

A class at Wick High School in 1958. Back row, left to right: Neil Gunn, Ian McGregor, David Gunn, Thomas Brown, Donald MacDonald, Alexander Calder, Donald Murray, Thomas Munro and Edward Gunn. Second back row: James MacKay, Robert Miller, Hazel Bethune, Lynne MacKain, Barrie Cormack, Isabel J. Mackay, Henry Grant and Peter Murray. Third row: Marella Swanson, Carol Whyte, Mary Alexander, Nancy Swanson, Lesley Hunter, Jacqueline Sutherland, Isobel A. Mackay, Margaret Gunn, Jessie Cormack, Helen Macleod, Brenda Turner and G. Anderson. Front row: Donald Macleod, Gordon Mackay, Andrew Calder, Robert Banks and Maxwell Mackenzie.   *Submitted by Hazel Lindsay.*

Teacher Miss Mackay keeps a watch over her charges of 1949/50 at Castletown Junior Secondary School. Back row, left to right: Donald Macleod, George Campbell, Angus MacLeod, Terence Mowat, William Coghill, George Anderson, Alexander Hossack, Hugh Crowden, Benjamin Geddes, James Younger, James Nicolson and Peter Wares. Second row: John Gunn, Robert Fulton, Alexander Swanson, Wilma Bruce, Christine Macleod, Jean Lyall, Virginia Geddes, Bettine Coghill, Anne Paterson, Marie Hill, James Gunn, John Sutherland and Leland Overy. Front row: Keith Murray, Jaye Sutherland, Sheila Sutherland, Jean Manson, Berta Farquhar, Marion Mackay, Anne Moodie, Rosemary Noble, Catherine MacPhee, Mary Gunn, Vanda ? and Elma Campbell.

Submitted by Denis Manson of Thurso.

Miss Lobban stands by her class of 1950/51 at Castletown Junior Secondary School. Back row, left to right: William MacPhee, Robert Fulton, John MacPhee, ? Morrison, John Sutherland, Alexander MacPhee and John Gunn. Second row: Hugh Crowden, Dennis Gunn, Mary Campbell, Catherine Macleod, Marie Hill, Iris Macleod, Virginia Geddes, Peter Wares and Alexander Swanson. Third row: Wilma Bruce, Berta Farquhar, Margaret Nicolson, Jessie Ogston, Elma Campbell, Daisy Hamilton, Catherine Hossack, Sheila Sutherland, Jaye Sutherland and Bettine Coghill. Front row: James Younger, James Moodie and Leland Overy.

Submitted by Denis Manson of Thurso.

Miss Swanson's class in the 1952/53 term at Castletown Junior Secondary School. Back row, left to right: Leland Overy, James Gunn, Donald MacLeod, James Younger, Martin Yolande, John Sutherland, Peter Wares, William Coghill, Terence Mowat, James Nicolson and Anthony Blunden. Second row: Hugh Crowden, Wilma Bruce, Marie Coghill, Iris MacLeod, Marie Hill, Jaye Sutherland, Bettine Coghill, Alexander Swanson and Robert Fulton. Third row: Elma Campbell, Berta Farquhar, Rosemary Noble, Marian Mackay, Anne Moodie, Mary Gunn, Jean Lyall, Sheila Sutherland, Virginia Geddes and Catherine MacPhee. Front row: John Gunn, James Moodie, Angus Macleod, George Anderson, Benjamin Geddes, George Campbell and Sandy Hossack.

Submitted by Denis Manson of Thurso.

Another Castletown school photo. Back row, left to right: William Inrig, Fraser Maclean, Donald Alexander, Brian Warner, John Gunn, Robert Murray, George Tait and Hamish Docherty. Second row: Thomas Stout, Robert Smith, Robert Paterson, Allan Robson, Denis Manson, Roderick MacKinnon, Gordon MacKenzie, John MacLean and George Robertson. Third row: Amy Munro, Sheena Mackay, Jean Gow, Iris Gunn, Margaret Humphrey, Janet Munro, Margaret Grant, Helen Watt, Helen Mackay, Barbara Gunn and Helen Adams. Front: Sybil Mackay, Fiona Cameron, Jocelyn Brown, Margaret Kennedy, Margaret MacKenzie, Margaret Ross, Linda Fraser and Nancy Watt.

Submitted by Denis Manson of Thurso.

Miss M. Swanson's Castletown class in the autumn of 1973. Back row, left to right: David Wallace, Susan Gunn, Lesley Bain, Fiona Henderson and Alan Nicolson. Second row: Charles Thomson, Sheena Sutherland, Lorna Gunn, Graham Younger, James Annal, Elizabeth MacPhee and Adam Auld. Front row: Susan Rhodes, Carol Mackenzie, Theresa Farmer, Donald Gunn, Alistair Steel, Veronica Fulton and Carol Keith. *Submitted by Mrs S. Keith of Castletown.*

Mrs Wilson and her pupils at Castletown, 1979. Back row, left to right: Mrs Wilson, Avril Grant, Patrick Gunn, Della Calder, Audrey Swanson, Donald Cormack, Martin Nicolson and Julie Mackay. Second row: Michael Custer, John Finlayson, Mandy MacDonald, Kevin Keith, Linda Calder, Deborah Fulton, Audrey Sinclair, Pamela Rhodes, David Shearer, Jacqueline Gunn and John Wares. Front row: Yvonne Campbell, Clive Fulton, Laura Logan, Norman Sutherland, John Baikie, Sharon Coghill, Fiona Sutherland and Sandra Budge. *Submitted by Mrs S. Keith of Castletown.*

This Pennyland Primary School photograph was taken in 1995. Back row, left to right: Alexander Wood, Sarah McAdie, Laura Wylie, Graham Christie, Thea Martin, Helen Anders, Ashley MacBeath, David Scott, Ricky Flowerday and Ryan Tait. Middle row: Matthew Maycock, Gary Porter, Stephanie Hutchin, Andrew Richardson, Marie Gunn, Ian Nicol, Katy Hepburn, Stacey Mackay, Kenneth Husband, Carly Sutherland and Jenika Mackay. Front: Irene Wares, Karen McColm, Glen Foster, Kirsty Rogers, Karen Black, Sarah O'Brien, John Sutherland, Laura Murdoch, Alan Watt, Leanne Sutherland, Marian O'Brien and Mark Harris.

Submitted by Sheilagh Tait.

Dunbeath school in 1980/81.

Submitted by Murdo Steven.

This Pennyland class photograph was taken in 1989. Back row, left to right: Julie ?, Janis Greg, John-Henry Harness, Clare Hughes, Jillian MacArthur, Neil Logie, Mark Macleod and Angela MacLean. Middle row: David Johnstone, Derek Peace. David Murray, Iain Scullion, Michael Tait, David McIvor and Gary Manson. Front row: Sarah Campbell, Shona Hay, Erin ?, Rhona McLennan, Lesley Ann, Audrey Chalmers, Vicki Munro and Jackie McGinlay. The teacher is Miss Swanson. *Submitted by Sheilagh Tait.*

Wick High School senior pupils gathering in the Norseman Hotel for a meal before going to the end-of-year prom.

Readathon, the BBC Children in Need appeal and the Julie Wheatcroft Trust each received generous cheques from pupils of Wick High School in 1996.

Money raised at the third-year and fourth-year disco and by a Wick High School MADD Society production was handed over to the special education unit at Pulteneytown Academy and to Blythswood Care in 1998.

Gala Week

Ronnie Fraser, whose display of flowers brightened up Wick's Market Place, came face to face with 'opposition' from a gala float.

Del Boy and Uncle Albert swapped Peckham for the streets of Wick and used their entrepreneurial skills to persuade local folk to part with their money at a gala week parade.

'Pirates of the Caribbean' sailed the seven seas to take part in the Wick Gala Week procession.

Bouncing babies from a Wick gala float.

These two Wick scorries came swooping down from the sky for a gala night parade.

Stalwart foot collectors Jenny Szyfelbain and her son Steven (left) and daughter Maura donned Viking gear for a gala procession.

Would you like to be given a bed bath by this nurse? Hospital high jinks on one of the Wick gala floats.

Maternity merriment on a Wick gala procession as an ambulance technician accompanies a giant-sized baby.

Colourful characters with their collection tins on the opening night of Wick Gala Week.

The scorrie nuisance in the town was highlighted on this Wick Gala Week float.

Wick's Royal Ascot float brought a touch of class to the gala parade. But was it a racing certainty to win a prize?

Hansel and Gretel on their gingerbread float tempted the Wick gala crowds to part with their pennies.

A tartan army taking to the streets of Wick as the Rob Roy movie is brought to life on gala night.

The Wonders of the World made a magic-carpet journey to adorn one of the Wick Gala Week floats.

A supersized scorrie was the centrepiece of this float on a Wick gala parade.

Meet the Rugrats as they prepare to go collecting on a Wick gala parade.

A Wick gala version of the Gills ferry – ready to brave the Pentland Firth!

Pikachu put in an appearance as a foot-collector during a Wick Gala Week parade.

These black-and-white harlequins provided a striking sight as they prepared to set off on the procession route through Wick.

Bill and Ben the Flowerpot Men – raising pots of cash for good causes on the opening night of Wick Gala Week.

A bouncing baby on one of the Wick gala floats.

'You're nicked!' Wick's new police station put in an appearance at the gala week children's fancy-dress parade at the Braehead.

This Rockwater towhead was specially constructed for Wick's gala procession.

Lining up on the starting grid, ready for a lap around the Braehead circuit, at the Wick children's fancy-dress parade.

The threat to Caithness General Hospital's maternity unit provided a topical theme for this Wick gala float.

Postman Pat and his black-and-white cat making a special delivery at Wick's Braehead.

Ready for the skirl of the pipes during the fancy-dress parade at the Braehead, Wick, a traditional part of the gala programme.

Magical characters impressing a large crowd on onlookers at the annual children's fancy-dress parade in Wick.

Little Weed, flanked by Bill and Ben the Flowerpot Men, making the most of the sunshine at Wick's Braehead.

Standing in line to impress the judges, these youngsters brightened up a summer evening at the Wick children's fancy-dress parade.

A host of colourful characters lining up at the Braehead for Wick Gala Week's ever-popular children's fancy-dress parade.

Bob the Builder was ready to tackle any job, no matter how big or small, at the Wick children's fancy-dress competition.

This young contestant at a Wick fancy-dress parade took comfort from a dummy while waiting to be judged.

The hippies of the Wick social security office had a groovy gala in 1985 when they won the supreme award.

Submitted by Alistair Sinclair of Wick.

Beautiful girls in a handsomely decorated horse-drawn cart. Daniel Sutherland has the reins in hand, though.
Submitted by Wendy Smith of Wick.

Wick's 1939 Herring Queen, Isabel Cormack, with her attendants Margaret Bremner (looking at camera), Isobel Bremner, Ina Hendry and Elizabeth Bain.
Submitted by Graeme Dickson of Wick.

Mary-Ann's Cottage – a history in pictures

Westside Croft at Dunnet was the home of Mary-Ann Calder until 1990 when, just before her 93rd birthday, she moved to a Wick nursing home.

Her grandfather, John Young, had built the cottage in the 1850s and the croft was successively worked by him, his son William, and finally by his granddaughter Mary-Ann and her husband, James Calder. Over three generations the way of life and working practices had continued largely unchanged.

Because of its historic nature, when the time came for Mary-Ann to leave the croft, she sought to have it preserved as it was – and so the Caithness Heritage Trust was formed to acquire the croft and carry out her wishes.

Professor Alexander Fenton, an authority on Scottish rural life, has written the following about Westside Croft:

'I have known about this croft for a long time. It is in its own right a most important social document. It incorporates in its layout and fittings a natural blend of the old and the new, showing how innovations and more modern concepts gradually displace or replace the old. In terms of field layout and details like the tethering of animals and the siting of plant-cots for cabbage-propagating on adjacent waste ground, there are rare pointers to the older, pre-improvement community system that prevailed throughout much of Scotland. It can be used, therefore, to interpret both the past and the more recent present, especially if it can be preserved with all its contents intact.'

The Trust restored the croft, as near as possible, to its state when last worked by Mary-Ann and James Calder. Since 1993, when it was officially opened by the Queen Mother, visitors have been taken on guided tours of the buildings during the summer months.

Mary-Ann died peacefully at her Wick nursing home on the eve of her 99th birthday in September 1996, but those who visit Westside Croft will find as they go round the house that her robust spirit still pervades the home where she lived for 90 years.

Mary-Ann's Cottage at Dunnet.

Mary-Ann's father, William Young (born in 1856), was the second son, and when he was fourteen he went to sea as ship's boy; for eight years he worked in local coasting and the Baltic trade. This was his sea-chest, and when it sailed for the first time on a large clipper, *The Westland* (inset), on her maiden voyage to New Zealand, a fellow seaman painted the picture of their ship in the lid of the chest. William eventually gave up the sea to run the croft.

The cottage living-room as it is now.

The Queen Mother holding the Magic Stone – a charm stone – as she listens intently to the story of its reputed healing powers.

James Calder was a crofter/fisherman. Surplus fish were salted and dried on this frame and stored for future use.

Andrew, great-grandson of Mary-Ann, visiting the croft at Westside, Dunnet. He is standing alongside a plaque marking the opening of the cottage by the Queen Mother.

The cottage front door with a plaque commemorating the Queen Mother's visit. Red was traditionally used for croft doors.

Mary-Ann's parents, William and Mary Young, all dressed up for this classic studio photograph.

Below: Mary-Ann by her fireside in 1989, the year before she moved to a Wick nursing home.

Great-grandson Paul Fitzsimmons is given a birthday tea by Mary-Ann on his ninth birthday in 1987.

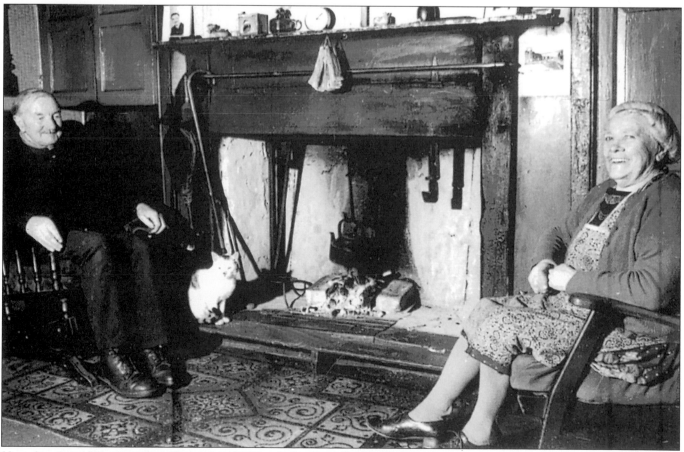

Mary-Ann (aged 86) and husband James (aged 97) by their cottage fireside in 1983.

J.P. Campbell.

William Young and his wife Mary with the newlywed couple
Mary-Ann and James in their Sunday best.

Mary-Ann (right) with sister Flora.

Mary-Ann, James and family members working at the peats.

William and Mary Young had eight children of whom three died in infancy. Pictured here are Mary-Ann (in front), her parents and her three sisters, Barbara, Flora and Lottie. On the right is her brother Jack who died as a teenager in the construction of Dwarwick House (now the House of the Northern Gate).

The agricultural college in Aberdeen periodically sent staff to Caithness to advise farmers and crofters on modern farming practices. This group of young women, at the outbreak of the 1914-18 war, were being trained in dairying. Back row, left to right: Bell Sutherland (Hunspow), Mary-Ann, Lizzie Manson, Greta Anderson, Katie Banks, Susie Begg, Bell Banks (one name missing). Middle row: Chrissie Young, Mandy Allan, Ellen Calder, Lizzie Oman, Winnie Sutherland (Barrock), Janet Henderson, Miss Malcolm, Miss Murray, Miss Ireland (Board of Agriculture dairy instructor, with cap). Front row: Barrie Brotchie and Chrissie ?.

Mary-Ann preparing pastry in her living room, which also served as kitchen and bedroom for over 100 years until a small purpose-built kitchen, with a water supply, was added in 1961.

National Museums of Scotland.

Right: Mary-Ann and James pause from haymaking in the 1930s.

When We Were Young

These youngsters were delighted to meet Santa at their Christmas party in the Pulteneytown Academy nursery in 1978.

A Children in Need fun day in Wick South Primary School saw head teacher Pat Bowers, dressed in a Pudsey Bear outfit, being encouraged by one of her pupils to crawl through the obstacle-course tunnel.

A cheer for head teacher Pat Bowers as she emerged triumphant in her Pudsey Bear outfit from the obstacle-course tunnel at a Children in Need fun day in Wick South Primary School.

A teddy bears' picnic was enjoyed by the Wick South Primary School nursery pupils.

These children in Miss Groat's class at Wick South wore their pyjamas to school on Children in Need day.

The Norlin Mothers and Toddlers welcome Santa to their Christmas party.

Hillhead Primary School in Wick hosted a group from AEA Technology and entertained them to a concert with a Scottish theme. Head teacher Ally Budge (left) is pictured with the pupils and guests.

'And here's a hand o' mine,' sang the children of Hillhead Primary School, Wick, when visitors from AEA Technology joined them for a mini-concert with a Scottish theme.

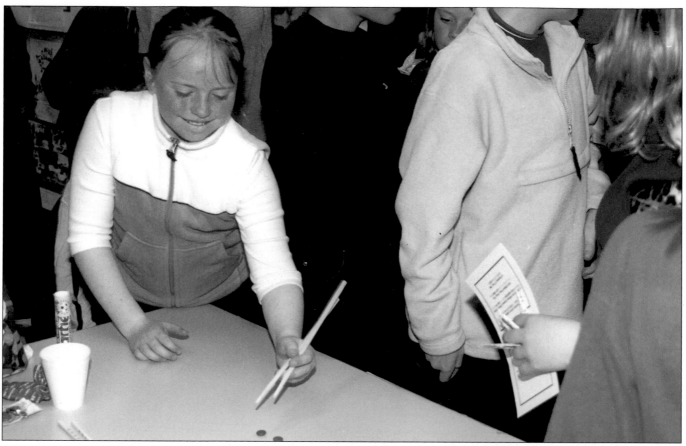

A study in concentration as this Hillhead pupil tries to use chopsticks during a special parents' evening.

The art of paper-folding was one of the intriguing attractions at a Japanese evening held in Hillhead Primary School.

Bonny Babies

A cheerful chappie waits for the judges
at a Wick Gala Week baby show.

Every one a winner at the baby show held as part of Wick's annual gala week programme.

Smiling faces all round at the Wick baby show, one of the main events of the annual gala week programme.

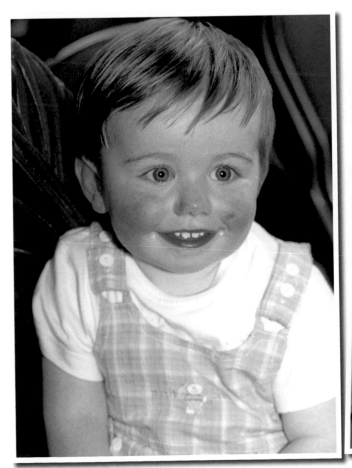

So happy to be part of the Wick Gala
Week baby show!

With the judges are the bonny babies who won prizes at the Lybster Gala Week baby show in the summer of 1981.

Senior Citizens and Volunteers

Smiles all round at the Wick senior citizens' treat in the Assembly Rooms. This popular event is always well attended, with friends meeting up for an evening of entertainment following a meal.

A greeting from Thomas Mackay, who helped run the Wick senior citizens' treat in the Assembly Rooms.

The January winds might blow, but the atmosphere in the Assembly Rooms was warm and welcoming when these Wick pensioners met up to share an evening of entertainment provided by the senior citizens' treat committee.

Hard at work in the kitchen of the Assembly Rooms in Wick are some of the volunteer helpers who worked hard to prepare an appetising hot meal for around 250 guests who attended the annual senior citizens' treat. This was the first time that the new crockery had been used.

Ready for a splendid evening's entertainment are some of the Wick senior citizens who enjoyed a night out at the treat.

Ready for an evening of hard work, serving and clearing up after the meal, are some of the willing volunteers who gathered in the Wick Assembly Rooms for the annual senior citizens' treat.

Major Graham Dunnett, Lord-Lieutenant of Caithness, accompanied the WRVS meals-on-wheels volunteers on their rounds to see for himself the invaluable service provided for pensioners who needed help in their own homes. The picture was taken in 1997 in Caberfeidh Court, where WRVS meals-on-wheels organiser Isobel Gates (standing, second left) was accompanied by two helpers, Muriel Ewing and Kathleen Gray.

Beenie Gray enjoyed having a dance with her nephew, former councillor Robert Durrand, at the senior citizens' treat in the Assembly Rooms, Wick, in 1999.

The Queen Mother and Family

With the sparkling waters of the Pentland Firth in the background, the Queen Mother and one of her corgis paused during a walk at the Castle of Mey.

The corgis were just as fond of the garden at the Castle of Mey when they joined the Queen Mother as she rested on the garden seat among the nasturtiums.

The Queen Mother made regular inspections of her Aberdeen Angus cattle when she was in residence at the Castle of Mey.

The Queen Mother spent years building up the prize-winning Aberdeen Angus herd of cattle at the Castle of Mey.

Even when she was nearing her centenary, the Queen Mother still loved to walk in her rose garden at the Castle of Mey.

Following the Queen Mother's death in 2002, the Royal Standard flew above the battlements of the Castle of Mey again when Prince Charles visited and officially unveiled a stone seat built in one of the Queen Mother's favourite places, outside the castle wall, where she liked to sit and watch the sunset over the Pentland Firth.

Entertaining guests in the drawing room of the Castle of Mey, the Queen Mother liked to invite them behind the chairs to look at the view over the Pentland Firth.

The Society of Caithness Artists visitors' book was signed every year that the Queen Mother attended the exhibition. A keen supporter of local artists, the royal visitor didn't miss many years during the regular visits she paid to the county.

Watched by Sister Kathleen Robertson, the Queen Mother signed the hospital visitors' book when she visited the Queen Elizabeth Wing of Caithness General Hospital in Wick.

A welcoming hug for Prince Andrew from the Queen Mother as the royal party, including the Queen, Prince Philip, the Duchess of York and her daughters Beatrice and Eugenie, arrived to spend the day at the Castle of Mey.

The Queen was always first to come ashore at Scrabster to be greeted by the Queen Mother.

The Queen Mother waving farewell to her family from the quay at Scrabster after they had spent the day with her at the Castle of Mey. On at least one occasion she went with them to have dinner on board the Royal Yacht *Britannia* before returning to the Castle of Mey later in the evening.

The Queen Mother's knowledge of plants was second to none. Her love of her garden at the Castle of Mey was obvious as she showed visitors how she had created it in the shelter of the high wall which gave it some protection against the strong easterly winds.

Accompanied by the Rev Tom Robertson, the Queen Mother shakes hands with church elder George Rosie before turning to speak to fellow elder Tommy Rosie at the end of a service in Wick Old Parish Church.

Leaving the refurbished Wick Old Parish Church with the Rev Stewart Frizzell.

Local photographer Janet McDonald lowered her camera for a moment to introduce her granddaughter Nadia and her mum Tanya McDonald to the Queen Mother as she was leaving morning service at Canisbay Church in 1999. Her Majesty remembered from a previous conversation that the baby had been born on Christmas Day.

93

A posy for the Queen Mother from Betty Sanders, a dedicated admirer and royal-watcher, who had travelled from the south of England to see Her Majesty on one of her annual visits to Caithness. The Queen Mother and her house guests had attended morning service in Wick Old Parish Church.

The Queen Mother was very pleased to meet the residents of Caberfeidh Court in Wick, where she is pictured chatting to Gladys Glander after the official opening of the Royal British Legion Scotland sheltered housing complex.

The Queen Mother chatting to Dunbeath girl Helen Lindsay, who was spending her summer holidays working in Dunbeath Heritage Centre, at the official opening.

The Queen Mother and her lady-in-waiting Ruth, Lady Fermoy, went for a trip on Thurso lifeboat after its naming ceremony.

A private visit to the gardens at Dunbeath Castle following the official opening of the village's heritage centre.

Lady Jessamine Harmsworth held parties in Thrumster House on several occasions during August to celebrate both her own birthday and that of the Queen Mother. Several of Lady Jessamine's many grandchildren are pictured with their grandmother and the royal guest of honour.

Thurso Pipe Band played for the Queen Mother at Mey Games. Her Majesty is pictured talking to well-known local photographer and piper John Macrae.

The Queen Mother chatting with the boys from an English public school who were invited to the Castle of Mey during the final leg of their Land's End to John O'Groats cycle relay in aid of Barnardo's, one of her favourite charities. The boys were treated to lemonade and chocolate cake before they set off again to complete the marathon.

Local policeman George Douglas proudly displays the Mey Games tug-of-war trophy which was won by the Castle of Mey team in 1980.

A handshake for the Castle of Mey tug-of-war team at the 1990 Mey Games.

Even at the age of 101, the Queen Mother was able to descend the aircraft steps unaided when she arrived at Wick.

Delighted to be back in Caithness in 2001, the Queen Mother waved to the crowd who had gathered at Wick Airport to greet her.

The Queen Mother chatted with Miss L. Bain (left) and Mrs A. Mackenzie who were guests at one of Lady Jessamine Harmsworth's parties at Thrumster House.

When she visited the Queen Elizabeth Wing of Caithness General Hospital, the Queen Mother chatted with (from left) Janette Doull, retired matron May Sutherland and retired nursing sister Wilma Taylor.

With a smile and a wave to the crowd, the Queen Mother is pictured leaving the Society of Caithness Artists' annual exhibition in Thurso to drive back to the Castle of Mey.

The Queen Mother drew quite a crowd when she opened the water plant at Hoy in 1955. *Submitted by Dennis Henderson.*

The ladies of Watten WRI made and presented a patchwork cushion to the Queen Mother when she opened the newly-refurbished village hall in 1973. *Below:* Meeting members of the hall committee at Watten.

Security was much more informal at Scrabster in the 1960s and '70s, with no barriers to keep back the crowds who gathered to see the Queen Mother as she chatted to Lord-Lieutenant John Sinclair while they awaited the arrival of the royal party from *Britannia*.

The Queen, as any mother would, extends a cautionary hand to make sure Prince Andrew doesn't fall into Scrabster Harbour.

With the Rev W. Nethercote Scott at Wick Old Parish Church.

The Queen Mother always made a point of attending morning service at churches in the county, and here she is leaving St Peter's Church in Thurso accompanied by her friends Commander and Lady Doris Vyner (first and second left).

An early visit to Canisbay Church.

The Queen Mother shaking hands with Vivienne Williamson before meeting some fellow members of Caithness Floral Art Club, along with representatives of the Society of Caithness Artists, at their annual exhibition in Thurso Town Hall.

Hettie Munro from the Ship's Wheel in Thurso was a long-serving stalwart member of the Society of Caithness Artists and she is pictured with the society's chairman, Hugh Leishman, and Mrs H. MacDonald as they toured the exhibition in Miller Academy, Thurso, with the Queen Mother.

Church Service

A stalwart of St Joachim's Church in Wick, Elsie Cabrelli was delighted when Bishop Mario Conti and Father John Symon called to see her in her home at Mount Hooley Terrace, Wick, in 1978.

The Christmas story was re-enacted by Wick Old Parish Church Sunday school members.

Children from all the Wick churches took part in an open-air Nativity play outside the post office in December 1976.

Leaving morning service in Wick Old Parish Church are (from left) Mrs C. Mowat, Beenie Gray, Nancy Buchanan, George MacDonald and Sheila Blackstock.

The ever-popular St Andrew's Holiday Club was a great hit with the dozens of youngsters who enjoyed a week of activities in 1978.

Wick Old Parish Church Youth Fellowship members took to the road on a sponsored cycle run. They are pictured outside the church hall being flagged off by the Rev Ian Stiven (right).

A poignant moment during a celebratory Mass in St Joachim's Church, Wick, as Sister Joseph renews her vows for the fiftieth time. A member of the Order of La Sainte Union, Sister Joseph had taught in secondary schools, as well as doing pastoral work in France and Zambia, before coming to Wick two years previously in 1978.

Under the direction of Peggy Barrett (pictured at the lectern, bottom left), a huge cast of Sunday school members performed a Nativity play in Wick Old Parish Church.

Wick Old Parish Church members, both young and not so young, held an Easter bonnet parade in the church hall in 1980. The entries were judged by Chrismay Leitch (back left).

Members of the Wick St Andrew's Church junior choir pictured with the Rev William Wallace in the new minibus they had helped raise funds for in 1978. The minibus was to serve the congregations of both St Andrew's and Thrumster churches.

Sister Joseph celebrated the fiftieth anniversary of taking her vows at a special Mass in St Joachim's Church, Wick. A member of the Order of La Sainte Union, Sister Joseph taught in the order's secondary schools in this country and also did pastoral work in Zambia and France before coming to Wick in 1978. A gift of a suitcase from the congregation was handed over by Simon Bowser and Colin Frame, with a little encouragement from Father John Symon.

111

Presentations and Celebrations

Quiet heroes: In 1975, constables Martin Bennis and David Anthony carried to safety an ice-factory worker who had been overcome with fumes. In the same year, William Banks had rescued a swimmer in difficulties in Wick Harbour. All three proudly displayed their Royal Humane Society certificates (in 1976), while the Wick harbour master, Captain Hamish Moore (right), was awarded a resuscitation certificate after an eight-year-old boy was pulled from the harbour. *Submitted by William Banks Junior of Wick.*

Donald Sutherland being presented with a gift for long service by manager Murdo Steven at the Pavilion cinema in 1976.

Submitted by Murdo Steven.

The official opening of the Rosebank Bowling Green, Wick in 1959. *Submitted by Graeme Dickson, Wick.*

It was quite a do at a Dounreay dance in 1958. From left to right the couples are Alex and Nancy Macadie, Daniel and Catherine Mackay, Harold and Dorie Barnes and Alan and Morag Macadie. *Submitted by Morag Macadie of Wick.*

Local staff of Pearl Assurance at their ball in 1963. *Submitted by Murdo Steven.*

Members of Keiss WRI visiting Bilbster. *Submitted anonymously.*

A Burns supper held by the Bower Young Farmers in 1965 at the Rosebank Hotel, Wick.   *Submitted by Allan Sutherland of Bower.*

These WRI ladies seem to be enjoying themselves in the Drill Hall in Wick in the early 1950s.

Submitted by Catherine Matheson of Wick.

Staxigoe Hall committee members and guest artistes who staged a Burns supper for the village residents.

A bath hoist was demonstrated by staff nurse Nan McMaster when it was presented to the old Bignold Hospital, Wick, before the move to the new Bignold Wing of Caithness General Hospital in the 1980s. It was accepted by sister Wilma Taylor, while other members of the nursing staff were (left to right) Marie Menzies, nurse Wendy Sutherland, staff nurse Linda Wares, staff nurse Margaret Maclean and nurse Ann Bremner.

The early bird catches the bargain. Shoppers gathered outside the Freezer Market when it was officially opened in 1984 in the building now occupied by the Citizens' Advice Bureau in High Street, Wick.

Members of the Wick branch of the Scottish Playgroup Association gathered to say farewell to Virginia Miller (seated, front centre) in the summer of 1979 and to thank her for all the work she had done on their behalf at local and national level.

All ready for a new season are members of the St Fergus Bowling Club, Wick.

Wick indoor bowlers celebrating a successful season with the presentation of their trophies in the Assembly Rooms in 1980.

Local postal staff gathered to say farewell to postmaster Tom Steven (seated, third from left) who was leaving in 1980 to take up a new job in Edinburgh.

Peter MacDougall congratulates incoming president Tom Buick as he hands over the Rotary Club of Wick chain of office in 1981.

The Caithness branch of the Scottish Playgroup Association held its 1980 AGM in Hillhead Primary School, Wick. Playgroups represented were from Bower, Dunbeath, Dunnet, Halkirk, Lieurary, Lybster, Reay, Thrumster, Watten and Wick.

Rocket-line apparatus was presented to Wick lifeboat by Jessie Alexander, of the town's Seaforth Avenue, whose nephew George Mackay had died earlier in 1978 in an accident on board the *Bengloe* at Jedda, Saudi Arabia. His fellow crew members started the fund to raise money for Wick lifeboat and the apparatus was accepted by coxswain Donald Mackay. The presentation followed a short service conducted by the Rev William Wallace and attended by friends and relatives of George Mackay and lifeboat personnel.

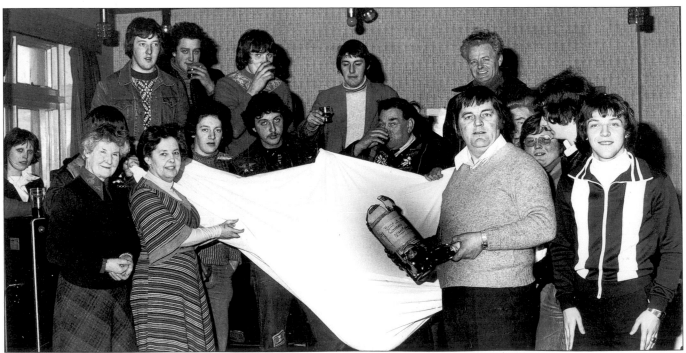

The contents of a large whisky bottle, filled with money donated by customers of the Inver Arms at Dunbeath, weighed down the sheet spread out to catch it when proprietor Murdo Steven performed the bottle-breaking ceremony. The money was donated to the local branch of a charity for people with learning difficulties.

Christmas 1978 saw a large gathering of Wick Luncheon Club members who enjoyed a festive meal in the town's youth club.

Wick Rosebank Bowling Club trophy-winners proudly displaying their silverware at their end-of-season dinner dance.

A Red Cross sale in the Assembly Rooms, Wick, in the spring of 1980.

In December 1969 the Bower Community Centre opened. This was the committee that had paved the way. Back row, left to right: J. Gunn, D. McLeod, D. Briggs, A. Coghill and W. Bremner. Front row: J. Sutherland, M. McAdie, D. McAdie, I. Mathieson, B. Henderson, C. Alexander, M. Cuthbertson, B. Mackay and C. Clyne. *Submitted by Sandra Coghill of Bower.*

Some of the many children who enjoyed an Easter party organised for them by Lodge St Fergus.

All ready for a three-hour hush-in are the lads of the East End Boys' Club of Wick, whose enforced silence raised a considerable sum for renovations to their clubrooms.

A scene at Wick station in May 1969. Friends and relatives of Thomas and Beera Scott have assembled to see them off, back to Vancouver after a Caithness holiday. Left to right: Jack Sinclair, Robert Sutherland, Lillibet Sinclair, Calder Sutherland, Robert Durrand, Hugh Gunn, William Gray and Christine Risbridger. *Submitted by J. Gunn of Wick.*

Soup, bread and cheese replaced the usual lunch in Mackay's Hotel for members of Wick Rotary Club when they raised money by having a 'hunger lunch' instead. President Bill Mackay (seated, left) and secretary Derek May (seated, right) were joined by (back, left to right) Henry Montgomery, Hugh Clark, Rob Sutherland, Bill Mowat, Gerry O'Brien, Magnus Sigurdsson and Hamish Maclean.

A reunion in the Lamplighter, Wick, for friends who attended Wick High School together. Back row, left to right: Jennifor Bruce (née Bruce), Eva Swanson (Smith), Janice Gibson (Miller), Jessie Bain (Budge), Mary McAdie (Swanson) and Rona Houston (Henderson). Front: Dorothy Pearson (Budge), Janet McDonald (Glander) and Margaret Telford (Ross).

Musical activities at Wick High School resulted in four cheques being presented to good causes.

This photograph of Keiss Youth Club was taken in 1984.

Dunbeath Football Club's dinner dance at the Rosebank Hotel in 1982.

Submitted by Murdo Steven.

A special hoist was presented in 1999 to the Wick multiple sclerosis group who were meeting each week for therapy sessions in Seaview House nursing home, under the direction of physiotherapist Anthea Macnee (fourth from left).

Caithness Car Club's dinner dance in 1995. Back row, left to right: J. Campbell, P. Miller, A. Jack, K. Dunnet, S. Coghill, D. Oag and A. Oag. Middle row: I. Malcolm, C. Smith, W. Ronaldson, A. Gunn, J. Ronaldson, D. Smith, B. Hamilton and W. Bremner. Front: W. Brown, J. Miller, G. Bremner, L. Munro, D. Manor, F. Oag and B. Oag. *Submitted by Sandra Coghill of Bower.*

The ribbon is cut to officially open the Wick Citizens' Advice Bureau premises in High Street in 1998.

Bower Young Farmers' winning junior speech-making team in 1983. They are Gordon Douglas (left), Sandra Sutherland and Kenneth Campbell. *Submitted by Sandra Coghill (Sandra Sutherland as was) of Bower.*

A gathering at the Pilot House in Wick in the early 1960s. *Submitted by Graeme Dickson of Wick.*

George Bruce receiving cheques from fireman Kenneth Swanson, Elizabeth Henderson (chair of Caithness Social Services Club) and Scott MacDonald of Wick North Primary School to boost the Caithness General Hospital radio service in 1986.

Submitted by Mrs Marie Sinclair (first on left in picture) of Wick.

129

Former Boy Scouts from all over the country gathered at Kirkhill, Wick, to unveil a plaque honouring much-respected Scoutmaster Johnny Yuill. The unveiling ceremony was performed by Cissie Mowat, whose late husband Alex had also been a Scoutmaster for many years.

Retiring after many years working in McAllan's Paint Shop in Bridge Street, Wick, Cathie Mackay received gifts and a bouquet, handed over by Jane Fraser, who with her husband Ronnie ran the shop. Other staff members in the photograph are (left to right) Jeanette Bain, Fiona Miller, Elizabeth Mackay, Karen Simpson, Jean Ferrier and Lynne Sutherland.

The Leith family from Wick raised a total of £2360 for Macmillan Cancer Relief in 1999. They are pictured with Wilma Swanson (fourth left) and Isobel Nicolson (fourth right), who accepted the cheque.

Office-bearers of the Order of the Eastern Star in 1981.

Members of the Inner Wheel Club of Wick celebrated their 25th anniversary by presenting a garden seat and money to refurbish the rose garden at Caithness General Hospital in June 1994. The cheque was handed over to Drew Macleod by the Inner Wheel president Janet McDonald.

Pipers and drummers from the Wick Girls' Pipe Band and their partners gathered for a reunion in the Rosebank Hotel in 1976.

Fred Gallagher and his wife Maria (seated, front centre) with staff of the local government buildings in Wick who held a retirement party for him in 1978.

Staff and families at Donald Sutherland's presentation at the Pavilion, 1976.

Submitted by Murdo Steven.

A plaque placed on the building in Harbour Terrace where Robert Louis Stevenson stayed during his time in Wick in 1868 was one of the quatercentenary year projects completed by members of the Wick WRI, who are pictured with Quatercentenary Queen Valerie Sutherland.

East End Boys' Club footballers, along with their friends and families, at the annual coffee evening in the Assembly Rooms, Wick, where the club's player-of-the-year awards were presented.

Office-bearers of the Order of the Eastern Star.

Wick Model Yacht Club members with their trophies for the season at the club's dinner dance in 1978.

The Entertainers

Winning teams of Wick Youth Club disco-dancers posing with their trophies.

Johnnie Sutherland (right) and Bobbie Murray performing at the Stardust Bar, Thurso, in 1984.   *Submitted by Graeme Dickson.*

Dunbeath's pantomime, *Cinderella*, in 1989/90.   *Submitted by Murdo Steven.*

Jennifer Magee playing the winning 'Song for Caithness' in 1972 to William Magee, who composed the piece.
Submitted by Mrs Nan Fraser of Canisbay.

Some of the Staxigoe Players of the 1950s – William Farquhar, Marie Farquhar, Sheila Ewing, Marie Sinclair, Winifred Mowat, Christine Mowat, Marie Ewing and Sheila MacDonald. *Submitted by Mrs Marie Sinclair of Wick.*

The popular Melotones of Thurso swinging in 1959. Left to right: Ross Taylor, Robert Forbes, Adam Polson and Denis Manson.
Submitted by Denis Manson of Thurso.

The Melotones played into the early sixties. This was a high school dance in 1959. *Submitted by Denis Manson of Thurso.*

The Coasters were a popular Thurso band from 1969 until the mid-seventies. This photograph shows them in action at the Viewfirth. Left to right: Denis Manson, Barbara Hunter, William Reid and George Thompson. *Submitted by Denis Manson of Thurso.*

The patrons of a Wick ATC coffee evening in the Assembly Rooms were well entertained by a visitor from the US base at Forss, who was in great demand during the time he was stationed in Caithness.

New Year Celebrations

Adding some sparkle to the occasion, this young lass and her mum were among the large crowd of revellers in Wick's Market Square for a New Year street party.

It was fun for all the family as the young ones were allowed to stay up and enjoy the Hogmanay celebrations in Wick town centre.

Dancing in Wick's Market Square to welcome in the New Year.
Below: The New Year was given an enthusiastic welcome by these revellers in Wick.

Our traditional Hogmanay celebrations were enjoyed by an overseas visitor as the pipers played in Wick's Market Square.

Scouts, Guides, Brownies, Rangers and Boys' Brigade

Thinking Day was held to celebrate 75 years of Guiding in 1985, and this smartly-turned-out foursome represented Caithness at the Royal Albert Hall in London. Standing at Thurso railway station are Girl Guide Alison Keith, Brownie Catherine Gordon, Guider Margaret Sheerin and Girl Guide Ruth Rosie. *Submitted by Mrs S. Keith of Castletown.*

Queen's Guide badges were awarded to Ranger Guide Vivien Vessey (left) and Linda Bruce of the 2nd Wick Company by District Commissioner Nettie Swanson.

143

A bouquet for Joan Lapwood after she had presented the trophies at the 1285 Caithness Squadron ATC annual inspection at their headquarters at Wick Airport. Mrs Lapwood's husband, Lionel, had been officer commanding the squadron in the 1950s.

The summer of 1978 saw the Wick Brownies and their leaders take part in an action song competition in Bower Hall which was judged by the county president, Lady Thurso (third left, back row), and branch president Margaret Turner (third right, back row).

Brownies take their places among the congregation in Wick Old Parish Church for a special service.

These men were all members of the 1st Wick Company Boys' Brigade when a company photograph was taken on their 50th anniversary in 1937. Half a century on, in 1987, they were delighted to pose for another picture in the BB Hall. Back row, left to right: Edward Tait, Frank Henderson, Alex Begg, Addie Henderson, Donald Sandison, Jack Banks and Angie Bain. Front: Donnie Mackay, Ben Campbell, Neil Mackay, Peter Ewing, Andrew Sinclair, 'Tiger' Macleod and Hugh Mackay.

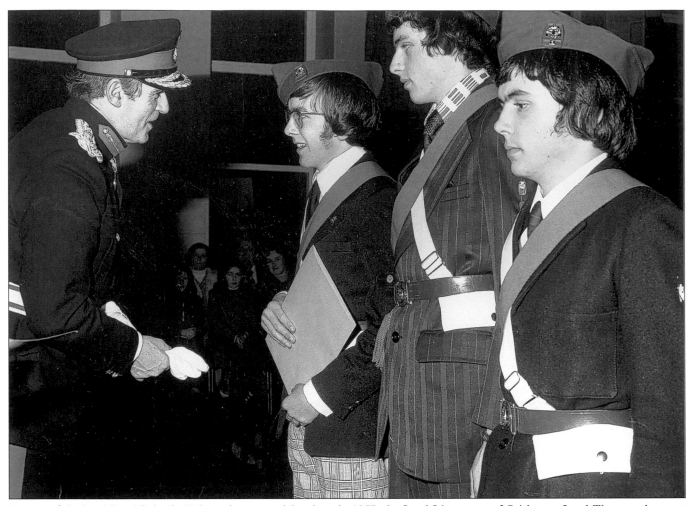

As part of the local Boys' Brigade 90th anniversary celebrations in 1977, the Lord-Lieutenant of Caithness, Lord Thurso, who went on to become the national president of the BB, handed over President's Awards to three sergeants – (left to right) Eon Cowie, Sandy Macleod and William Moore – at a ceremony in the Assembly Rooms, Wick.

A souvenir photograph of the Wick Scouts and Cubs when they moved to their new hall at Kirkhill from their original headquarters at Harrowhill in 1980.

146

Douglas Campbell, of Breadalbane Terrace, Wick, received the Chief Scout Award from District Commissioner Peter Cadman (left), watched by Scout leader Robert Duncan, in 1984.

A fancy-dress competition for Girl Guides and Brownies in the Parish Church hall.

Wick and Keiss Guides gathering outside the Bridge Street Church hall for a clean-up of Wick's riverside area in June 1976.

A group of Ranger Guides in Wick taking part in a course on car maintenance in 1988.

Above: All ready for a clean-up around the town in 1980 are the girls of the 3rd Wick Guides, who used to hold their meetings in Wick Old Parish Church hall.

Left: Having been saving their coppers, these Wick Brownies made a mile of pennies for charity in March 1978.

Let's Have a Party

Having a grand night at the Rosebank Hotel in 1970.

Submitted by Allan Sutherland of Bower.

The Dolphin Restaurant was the venue for a staff function for workers from the stocking factory at the airport run by Mr Brunton. The picture was taken in January 1952.

Submitted by Morag Macadie of Wick.

Another picture from the stocking factory workers' night out.   *Submitted by Morag Macadie of Wick.*

Stocking factory staff enjoying their social gathering in the Dolphin Restaurant in 1952.   *Submitted by Morag Macadie of Wick.*

A children's party in 1957/58 at the Station Hotel, Wick.

Submitted by Wendy Smith of Wick.

It was Coronation Day and a new sovereign was on the throne. Donald Dunnet, William Bremner and William Allan lead the celebrations outside the Castle of Mey.

Submitted by William Magee of Lower Gills.

Gifts for Lady Jessamine Harmsworth at
her 80th birthday bash in 1990.
Submitted by Graeme Dickson of Wick.

On Parade

With cameras at the ready, the crowd in Bridge Street, Wick, wait patiently to see the spectacle of the massed pipe bands in 2000.

Wick Town Centre Events Group and helpers were ready to lead the Christmas parade through the town to the Market Square.

Santa was soon surrounded by happy children when he visited Wick's Market Square.

It was jingle bells all the way through Wick town centre as Santa arrived on his reindeer-drawn sleigh.

The sun shone on these young contestants in an Easter bonnet competition as they were interviewed by Lorna Simpson in Wick's Market Square.

Taking time off from Saturday afternoon shopping in Wick to watch the Easter bonnet parade.

Farmyard animals, ponies, chickens, ducks and geese attracted a large crowd at an animal farm day organised by the Wick Town Centre Events Group.

An enthusiastic audience enjoying the entertainment in Wick's Market Square on a sunny Saturday afternoon.

The Wick RBLS Pipe Band acquired two extra members, in the guise of Lorna Simpson and Marie Gilmour, when they marched along High Street to join the festivities in the Market Square.

Young and old alike congregating in the town centre to watch a parade by Wick RBLS Pipe Band.

Cock o' the North at the Wick RBLS Pipe Band fancy-dress parade.

These youngsters decided to don fancy dress themselves to collect money for the Wick RBLS Pipe Band when the pipers and drummers disguised themselves in eye-catching costumes for the final parade of Pipe Band Week.

Drumming up support for Wick Pipe Band, when they held one of their very popular parades in the Market Square.

Gone Fishing

Robert Carter on the *Silver Cloud* in the mid-sixties.

Submitted by Keith Macadie of Wick.

George and Robert Carter on the *Silver Cloud* in the sixties.

Submitted by Keith Macadie of Wick.

Young Richard Macadie at sea on the *Strathdonan* in 1995.
Submitted by Keith Macadie of Wick.

Young Keith Macadie on his grandfather's boat *Spindrift* in 1967.
Submitted by Keith Macadie who is now slightly older but never escaped to sea and is still in Wick.

Wick's fishing heritage is solidly based on the silver darlings. George More, William Sutherland and Michael Durrand are working on George's boat, the *Chance*.

Submitted by Morag Macadie of Wick.

William Tait (seated) and James Oag have a crack with a suited gentleman as they relax beside the *Morning Star* in the mid-seventies.

Submitted by Allan Tait of Wick.

Angus Gunn, over on holiday from America, fishing at
Longberry – and successfully, it would appear.
Submitted by J. Gunn of Wick.

Geoff Maynard (left) and Billy Swanson aboard the
creel boat *Deo Volente* at Scrabster in 1993.
Submitted by Graeme Dickson of Wick.

Sailing across the Pentland Firth to Stroma in the summer of 1991.

Submitted by Graeme Dickson of Wick.

All in a Day's Work

Postie William Cormack has a quick break while awaiting the post van in 2006.

Gordon Spence (getting into car) with some of his workforce outside his electrician's shop at Harbour Quay, Wick, in 1982.

Submitted by Graeme Dickson of Wick.

Fountain Forestry workers at Loch More in 1981. *Submitted by Graeme Dickson of Wick.*

Alexander Budge with Sweep and Meg, in front of a huge mound of peat stacked at Auckengill in 1974.

Submitted by Mr C. Budge of Nybster.

Staff of the Wick Dental Practice pictured in the Francis Street dental surgery.

The staff and those connected with Headlines hair studio in 1985.

Submitted by Sandra Coghill of Bower.

Staff at Four Seasons in
Dempster Street, Wick,
making a floral display
in the summer of 1986.

1978 saw the Sutherland family from Achardle hard at work making furniture.

The changing face of Wick's High Street as the old buildings are bulldozed.

Pictured tidying up after a busy Save the Children Fund thrift shop in 1980 are local members (left to right) Mrs M. Lamont, chairwoman Mrs J. Lapwood, Mrs J. Sutherland, Mrs P. Weir, Mrs M. Sutherland and Mrs M. Baikie.

Mike Burnett (second left), president of the Scottish NFU, presented Agricultural Training Board certificates to (from third left) Donald Campbell, Upper Milton; Ian Gunn, Whitefield; John MacAdie, Lieurary Mains; James Mackay, Aimster; Alan Murray, Bilbster; and Leslie Robertson, Braeval. Also in the picture is Donald Coghill (left), Stemster Mains, chairman of the apprenticeship committee for Caithness and Sutherland.

David Campbell, of Rosebery Terrace, Wick, opened a cycling shop in Glamis Road in the 1980s, selling everything from sophisticated racing bikes to washers.

Trainees on a hospitality course in the Mercury Motor Inn, Wick, listen intently to their instructor in 1978.

Owners and staff at Allan's of Gillock in 1986.

Submitted by Sandra Coghill of Bower.

Caithness Pets

All the trophy-winners at the 73rd annual show of the Caithness Ornithological and Fur Society in the Assembly Rooms in 1978.

A dog show at the Assembly Rooms, Wick. The weather was so warm that the event was moved outside.

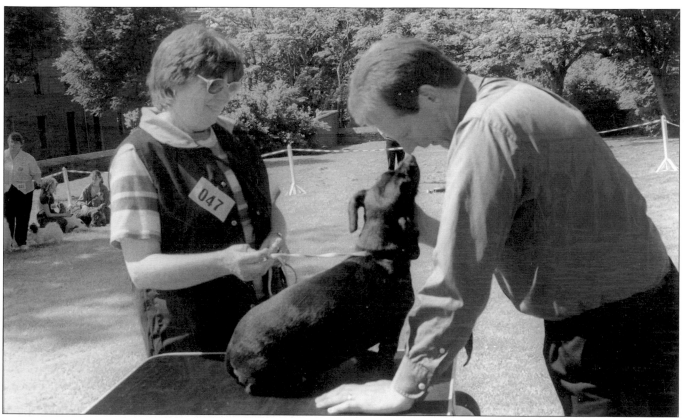

A hopeful canine at the dog show at the Assembly Rooms.

These golden retrievers are the latest in the generations that have greeted customers at Bamber's Bridgend Service Station, Thurso, for over twenty years. Tasha is sitting, while Hollie contemplates life from a prone position.

Submitted by Alan Bamber of Thurso.

173

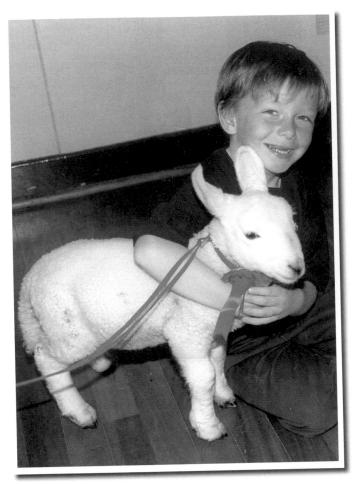

Love me, love my lamb... The judges did, because they awarded him a first prize at a pet show in the Assembly Rooms.

This purrfect pet won a first prize at the Caithness fur and feather Show in the Assembly Rooms.

Happy to have a cuddle, this kitten didn't know what all the fuss was about at the Wick pet show.

Cowboy and canine Indian at the dog show held at the Assembly Rooms, Wick.

Face to face with a long-eared owl in 1977.
Submitted by Graeme Dickson of Wick.

Tommy Mackenzie inspects a herring-gull chick in 1977.
Submitted by Graeme Dickson of Wick.

Fur and feather judge Jessie Doull preparing to hand over a trophy to a young competitor at a Wick show.

We Will Remember Them

Pipe Major Bobby Coghill leading members of the Royal British Legion Scotland to a service of remembrance in the war graves section of Wick Cemetery.

Paying tribute to the fallen of two world wars at the war memorial in Wick on Remembrance Sunday.

Led by Major Alan Ferrier, members of the Wick branch of the Royal British Legion Scotland make their way to Wick Old Parish Church for a service of remembrance.

As a shaft of autumn sunshine streams through the stained-glass windows of Wick Old Parish Church, the Rev Stewart Frizzell accepts the RBLS standard at the start of a service of remembrance.

Wreath-bearers marching to the war memorial in Wick in 1987.

Crowds gather round the Wick war memorial to watch Lord Thurso lay the wreath of behalf of the Queen in 1976.

Caithness Characters

It's not everyone who can say they've been mauled by a lion at Wick's Riverside and lived to tell the tale. This is William Harper, recovering in the Bignold Hospital following the incident at a visiting circus in 1981. The lion was put down.

Submitted by Graeme Dickson of Wick.

Punk rocker Maurice McLeod in Thurso in 1985.

Submitted by Graeme Dickson of Wick.

George Robertson of Wick in 1980.
Submitted by Graeme Dickson of Wick.

Cabrelli's Cafe, run by Louis and Pina, is now a distant Wick memory. Here Jack McPhee, Alexander Mackay and Alistair Malcolm gather in front of it in April 1981.
Submitted by Graeme Dickson of Wick.

Showtime

Having a closer look at some of the machinery at the 1978 County Show held at the Riverside, Wick.

Staff of Macrae & Dick manning their stand at the County Show at the Riverside, Wick, in 1978.

John Sutherland stands with groom Tracy Barnie at the 1994 County Show. George Ronaldson and David More are the coachmen.
Submitted by John Sutherland of Wick.

These green-fingered folk won the trophies at a Wick flower show in the Assembly Rooms.

Our heritage

Wick Society member William Lyall had the task of framing and restoring the pictures that were to go on display in the heritage centre for the 1980 summer season.

1980 saw a hive of activity in the Wick Heritage Centre as the volunteers worked hard to get it ready to open for public viewing. Architect Stuart More (right) was responsible for planning the layout of the various displays and he is pictured discussing one of the plans with Norman Crowe.

All hands on deck in 1980 as Wick Society members try to manoeuvre the Stroma yawl they had acquired for their exhibition in the heritage centre.

It was a dream come true for Wick Society chairman Iain Sutherland (left) as he got ready to accept the keys of the Wick Heritage Centre from Councillor Tom Pollok, chairman of the leisure and recreation committee of Caithness District Council. Three years before, in 1977, the district council had decided to convert two derelict houses in the Telford-designed area of Lower Pulteney as a new home for the Wick Society's museum and, with assistance from the Manpower Services Commission, this ambitious scheme was nearing completion. The society, which had gathered a vast amount of material relating to the fishing industry, then faced the task of sorting and cataloguing the exhibits and hoped that the museum would be open by the end of 1980. The premises included a courtyard, a fish-curing kiln and a boat-house, with a gallery added to allow visitors to view the vessels from above. Other facilities to be available to the public were a small art gallery, a kitchen, toilets, a reception area and a shop. A photographic darkroom had also been provided for use by the Wick Society. The Caithness stone buildings had been restored with great care and this meant part of the centre being reroofed with flagstones.

Game On

Wick Model Yacht Club celebrated its golden jubilee in 1976. The winners of two trophies that day, including the Golden Jubilee Cup itself, were Andrew Sinclair (on the left), father Drewie Sinclair and the contributor Alistair Sinclair. They are pictured outside the club hut at Loch Sarclet.

This group photograph was taken during Wick Model Yacht Club's golden jubilee year, 1976.

Submitted by Allan Tait of Wick.

Model yachts on a summer's day on Wick River.

Submitted by Alistair Sinclair of Wick.

Ready, steady... One of the races at a Keiss school picnic in the early 1950s. Left to right: C. Campbell, J. Rosie, I. Bain, D. Galleitch, M. Sinclair, M. Cormack and N. Leitch. Miss Budge the teacher is looking on, and behind her is J. Sinclair. *Submitted anonymously.*

From the same school picnic, this was the sack race. The lady with her hand over her face is unknown but, left to right, the picture shows N. Leitch, A. Macleod (teacher), C. Campbell, M. Cormack, D. Galleitch and J. Taylor. *Submitted anonymously.*

A model yacht race is about to begin at Loch Sarclet in the 1960s.   *Submitted by Alistair Sinclair of Wick.*

Wick Motorcycle Club members in 1963. J. Mackay is presenting a cup at the coastguard quarry. The riders are (left to right) G. Forbes, William Doull, Robert Watts, William Stewart, Donnie Plowman, James Plowman, Bruce Tait, Alex Mowat, J. Johnstone and Iain Harper.   *Submitted by James Plowman of Wick.*

A team photo – thought to be a rural select – from the time when the changing rooms at the Naver pitch in Thurso were opened in the early 1970s. Back row, left to right: J. Magee, C. Cameron, A. Manson, C. Swanson, G. Harris and A. Sutherland. Front row: A. Macleod, J. Robertson, N. Banks, H. Gunn, A. Mowat and D. Manson. *Submitted by Allan Sutherland of Bower.*

An East End football team with their coaches. *Submitted by Morag Macadie of Wick.*

Players of the year from the East End Boys' Club in 1980 were (left to right) Ian Coghill, William Taylor, Liam Ross and John Inglis. The shields were presented by East End vice-president Jock More (right) and the coaches for the various age groups were (back row, left to right) Wilfred Budge, James Bremner, Jack Harper and Allan Lannon.

Thurso Pentland Boys' Club under-12s won the William Sinclair Memorial Trophy in 1978. It was handed over by Bill Ward, regional director of the Scottish Association of Boys' Clubs, from Edinburgh. Pentland beat a team from East End Boys' Club 3-2 at Wick's Bignold Park.

Footballers from East End Boys' Club after a match at Wick's Riverside in the 1970s.

A victorious team from East End Boys' Club under-12s in 1978.

Provost Morton Smith of Thurso with the winning team (all from Halkirk) in a five-a-side football tournament – (left to right) James Gunn, Michael MacDonald, Peter Mackay, Neil Mackay and Robert MacDonald. *Submitted by Mrs Rosalind Falconer of Halkirk.*

Four members of the Rotary Club of Wick – (left to right) Clair Manson, Jim Mackenzie, Colin Terris and Donald Miller – trying their hand at target shooting under the watchful eye of instructors Alex Mowat (left) and Douglas Sutherland.

In the Dundee Games of 1976 Caithness was represented by Gordon MacDonald (in third) and Victor Polanski (in seventh).
Submitted by Gordon MacDonald of Wick.

A cycling race at the 1977 Caithness Highland Games in Thurso – (left to right) James Mackay, Michael MacDonald, Raymond MacGregor, George MacKenzie, Richard Polanski, Michael Gray, John Polanski and Andrew Simpson.
Submitted by Gordon MacDonald of Wick.

A determined Fiona Douthwaite at the 1977 Caithness Highland Games in Thurso. *Submitted by Gordon MacDonald of Wick.*

Donald Carmichael at Reay in 1923. *Submitted by Gordon MacDonald of Wick.*

Wick cyclist Gordon MacDonald arriving at the Nethercliffe Hotel, Wick, with Brian Grant and Brian Kennedy who accompanied him on a sponsored cycle from Inverness to Wick to raise funds for BLISS (Baby Life Support Systems). Left to right: Brian Grant, Donnie Grant, Valerie Cook, Willie Mackay, Gordon MacDonald, Alice Kennedy, Brian Kennedy, Denis Hill, Marilyn Nicolson and Hilary Hill. Gordon managed a creditable time of seven hours, 14 minutes and 45 seconds. *Submitted by Gordon MacDonald of Wick.*

All set for the start of the Keiss school picnic wheelbarrow race. Back row, left to right: N. Leith, J. Dunnet, J. Swanson and D. Galleitch. Front row: N. Harrold, S. Bain, H. Fraser and C. Cormack. *Submitted anonymously.*

Under-fives warming up for their race at the 1954 Keiss school picnic – (left to right) G. Steven, W. Bain, B. Dunnet, A. Mackay, J. Robertson, D. Dunnet, J. Mowat, M. Alexander and M. Cormack. The adults are L. Mowat and J. Mowat. *Submitted anonymously.*

Caithness Highland Games day in Thurso in 1975: Gordon MacDonald leads from William Bain, with James Duff hidden and Robert Duff and Victor Polanski pursuing. *Submitted by Gordon MacDonald of Wick.*

Gordon MacDonald with some of the rising stars of the local cycling scene. *Submitted by Gordon MacDonald of Wick.*

East End stalwarts James Bremner (back, left) and Jock More with some of their young footballers at the Bignold Park, Wick.

Coach Wilfred Budge with an East End Boys' Club team in 1975.

The Dunbeath football team of 1982.   *Submitted by Murdo Steven.*

Seaforth Avenue FC, season 1984/85. Back row, left to right: Dougie Bremner, Raymond MacDonald, Stephen Fraser, David John, Andrew Carter, Andrew John, Glyn Reid. Front row: Victor Risbridger, Willie Cowie, Graham John, Denny MacDonald, Kevin Beales, Andrew Taylor.   *Submitted by Mrs and Mrs R. MacDonald of Wick.*

Marksmen from Wick Old Stagers Rifle Club proudly displaying their individual and team trophies for 1990. Back row, left to right: Taco Nolf, James D.M. Sinclair, Graeme Sutherland, A.J.K. Mowat, William Ronaldson and William Simpson. Front: Clair Ronaldson, Hugh Simpson Jnr, Hugh Simpson Snr and Allan W. Paul. *Submitted by Mrs Marie Sinclair of Wick.*

The Wick Model Yacht Club dinner dance in 1976, celebrating its jubilee year. *Submitted by Alistair Sinclair of Wick.*

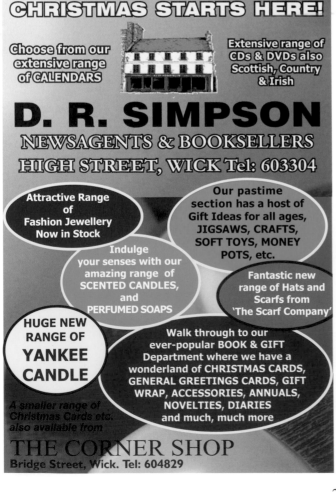
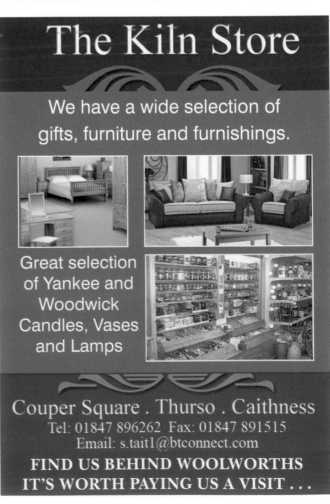

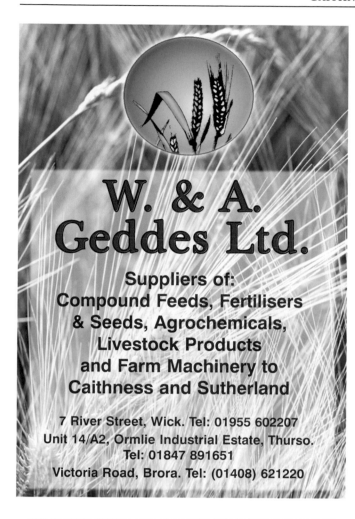

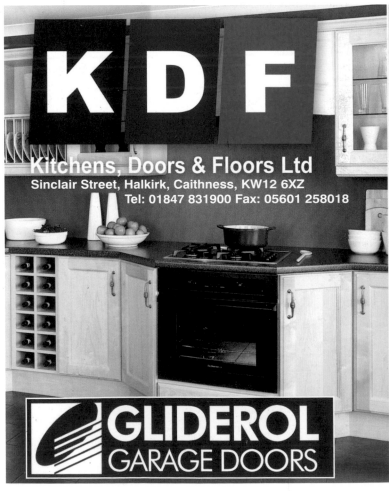